What Trees Know

For Carol & Mohammed —
Dearest friends

Emilio DeGrazia

What Trees Know

Emilio DeGrazia

NODIN PRESS

ACKNOWLEDGMENTS

Initial publications include: "Tuesday Serenade" as ("Serenade") in *Turtle Quest,* 2009. "How to Turn the Other Cheek," *Plainsongs,* 2019. "What Leaves Know," *Italian Americana,* 2008. "Phantom Pain," "What Roots Know," "Know-Nothing," "Living Outside-In," "Winter's Fall," "Spring Cleaning," appeared in various issues of *The Green Blade,* 2009-13. "What Leaves Know," "Jesus and His Tree," "Good Friday," "After the Logging," and "Summer Storm" were previously published in *Seasonings* (Nodin Press, 2012). "Burying the Tree" initially appeared in *Burying the Tree* (Plain View Press, 2006) and was reprinted in *Walking on Air in a Field of Greens* (Nodin Press, 2009). Thanks to Aaron Haley, Plainview, for his artwork (opposite page) featuring tree and bicycle.

SPECIAL THANK YOU

To Monica DeGrazia, my beloved spouse, for her dedicated support and sound literary advice.
To Dante Carmine DeGrazia, my son, for his passionate devotion to music and for his partnership in our "What Trees Know" words and music performances in Minnesota and beyond.
To Norton Stillman, publisher of Nodin Press, for his decades of dedication to Minnesota authors.

9 8 7 6 5 4 3 2 1

ISBN: 978-1-947237-27-8
Design: John Toren
Library of Congress Control Number: 2020942104
Printed in USA

Nodin Press, LLC
5114 Cedar Lake Road
Minneapolis, MN
55416

www.nodinpress.com

This work is dedicated
to Dean Harrington
(April 29, 1949–February 2, 2019)
and Sally Harrington
with gratitude for their support of theatre, literature
and the arts, and the proper use of land.

TAKE NOTE

People have a prejudice against what's low-down deep, silent and slow, and they're hooked on looking up.

– Posthumous, 753 BCE

Table of Contents

VI. The Giving Tree

VII. Burying the Tree

I

THE SECRET LIFE OF TREES

Believe me, you will find more lessons in the woods than in books. Trees and stones will teach you what you cannot learn from masters.

   – St. Bernard of Clairvaux, *Epistola*

No knowledge is ever lost; nothing can ever be forgotten. Carefully held by the trees, the memory of our knowledge is continually scribed by the land. How do we know it once more?

   – Monica Gagliano, *Thus Spoke the Plant*

KNOW-NOTHING

The secret is all mine:
Ripples on shorelines of seas
Say nothing clear to me—
So I can't make sense

Of those fish schools
Lurking big-eyed below
Weaving their way like dreams
As they swim in my mind.

And I can't stare down
The sun that glares
Its fires at me so brilliantly—
To see how it sees me,

Or know what light it can shed
On war, suffering or love,
Or why the laziest leaves
Of autumn trees keep hanging on,

Or why trees never hold jobs
Or run away, and never complain
That their heartwood is unseen
From the windshields of cars,

Or why trees, unlike lords and priests,
Invent no theories and theologies—
Flowering, swaying, still and moved,
Airing and beautiful.

ASPEN VERSE

Only connect...
    – E.M. Forster, *Howard's End*

If everything…this life…
Were made of dots,

The prophet would understand
Why braided aspen roots

Shudder the surface of a pond
While the traffic in L.A. is touched

By the whiskers of a catfish
Brushing weeds in deepwater murk—

And why no thoughts shimmer
Up and down finger spines

As hands make music
In black and white on piano keys,

And why melodies self-organized
Into wordless symphonies

Scatter fishlet schools
Away from the shadows of sharks.

In the pauses between breaths
Aspen roots weave embroideries

Envied by artists in Paris and New York
And not for sale in the marketplace.

"You may never know," the aspens whisper,
"What you may learn from us today."

WHAT LEAVES KNOW

The power of place,
Their role
In the dazzling outcome of roots.

The art of living within view
Of the two fragrances of life,
Sun and shade.

The politics of free passage
For air allied to no state.
The turn the other cheek tactic
For storms gone wild.

How to brew the air we crave.

How to orchestrate
The incomparable music
Composed by anonymous winds.

Leaves know how to sway
And dance,
How to put their colors on,
Blaze away, be

Outward and visible signs
Of a big beautiful thing
Wonderfully in the way.

On foggy still nights
They know the atonement of sleep,

The moment to let go.

BUSINESS AS USUAL

While landlord priests build malls
And walls out of paper and prayers,

Mycelial networks keep their peace
About what's good for creeping things.

I have yet to see a snake dance a hymn
In praise of the rainbows on her skin,

Or hear a dolphin, sting ray or shark
Or dragonfly above a lily pad

Or bees nosing an apricot bud
Pray for the salvation of money or souls.

The hum in water, air and dirt is busywork
Prayer rarely heard outside the walls

Where leaves whisper sweet nothings to winds
And roots secrete moisture across property lines.

ORCHESTRATION

From his perch on the porch
He calls time out to tune in
The harmonics of the undertow
Directing the river downstream,

While vibratos performed in forests
By breezes over fine-tuned leaves
Move the sky to play chords
Only insects feel.

SONG-LIFE

After his sister, Aurora, passed away,
She who played the old upright and sang,
Her melodies hovered like an aura
Sunsetting light in his living room.

When she lay dying he felt the slow fall
Of the rhythms of her breaths, the air
He held in whenever the mailman appeared
As shadow before his front door.

Evenings he keeps recalling her melodies
And conjures the colors of the dress
She wore the night she spun into the arms
Of the man who loaned her his name,

And how after she married him
And retreated into the noise of years,
Her piano became her confidant
And only lover in the house.

What did the lumber in that upright
Take in from her fingers and voice?
What melodies did it memorize
When she played and sang them again?

One night when they were alone in their beds
The two men—haulers who pitched the piano
From their truck into a dumpster ditch—
Were awakened by the gravity of its last chord.

WHAT ROOTS KNOW

And what do roots know—
Their eyes mud-smeared in the dark?
How do they decide it's time again
To burrow their way down, purl

More deeply toward the succulence
Of moisture and minerals that ascend
To unfurl in sky like prayers
Unleaving from autumn trees?

Eons ago what tangle of root DNA
Spiraled forth to become the forest clans
That crossed mountains and seas
To be hewn into shelters where we live

And toil cross-eyed in midnight oil,
Inscribing our whims on Bible leaves
While re-engineering the genius of genes
Into our manuals and machines?

The grammars of what lost languages
Inform tendrils and taproots
Wise enough to translate their alchemies
Into trunk, branches, flowers and fruit?

Listen dearly to the chords
Pianos exhale from wood deemed dead,
And to roots taking tones in from dirt.

TEXTING

A whiff of apples fermenting on grass
Dizzies murmuring minds
Wide-eyed under clear midnight skies.

Below that starlight minnows glide
In streams with waves of sound
Deaf to the moans of holy books
Deconstructing in the silt of caves.

There, where the elements
One day will remainder us
With senseless debris, words
Calcified by paper and ink

Dissolve into moisture and earth,
Their breaths exhaled into roots
Busy inscribing ancient hieroglyphs
On the ribwork of new leaves.

THE WAY HOME

His boots fit his tracks best this way—
As if he can see where he's going
By retracing the trail his years made in the dark
Down the sidewalk and across the street
Into the out-of-sight years disappeared
In playgrounds and schools, with the church
On the far end of town looking down,
Indifferent to stars on a moonless night
Casting their shadows on the white.

The snow comes down thick and warm,
And covers the tracks farthest from home—
The silos and baseball field, the railroad ties
Leading to his first kiss by the riverside,
And to the bookstore, its eyes boarded up.

The tracks in snow know the way home
To what's faithfully luring him on—
His wife worried and wondering,
The small room, the light next to his chair,
And there, outside the window, the moment
And the future he looks forward to
Whenever he gazes at the old oak—
Gnarled and rough—whispering to him
About dignity, stability, beauty and peace.

BLIZZARD BRIDE

In the prairie blizzard the distant trees
Are bent and bare—like hunched tribes

Wandering in search of villages
Lost in the death shroud of a hurricane.

Behind windows farmers watch and wait
For the madness of atheist winds to morph

Into the white noise that broods
Over fences, roofs and fields

Until sun, in a sky suddenly blue,
Casts a silvery spell on the crowns of trees.

Here corn stubble aligned in soldier rows
Gleams more pallidly than Arlington stones.

Beneath this expanse, this blank sheet,
Earth seems in control, composed,

Waiting for the whispers of breezes
To lift a bridal veil from her face.

Listen to this silent loveliness, she says.
In it I hear a distant hunting horn

And feel the old vibrato of lust
Shivering the naked limbs of trees.

II

A WEEK'S WORTH OF TREES

Can only those hope who can talk?

    – Oliver Wendell Holmes (1841-1935)

The tree which moves some to tears of joy is in the eyes of others only a green thing that stands in the way.

    – William Blake (1757-1827)

And in general the bodies of the trees, as of other living things, have in them skin, blood, flesh, sinews, veins, bones and marrow.

    – Pliny the Elder, *Natural History* (d. 79 CE)

MONDAY BUSINESS AS USUAL

So what are they saying today,
Without muddling the scene with words—
Today, my morning Monday leaves,
The maple's maroons and greens
Sun-shined in rainbow veins,
The cottonwood snowing in June,
And black locust lacework of leaves,
The poplar's shimmering in sun,
The hickory, hackberry and oak,
Dogwood, willow and birch,
The pine, chestnut and fir,
Ash, walnut and elm,
The softhearted butternut—
All rooted, fresh airing the neighborhood
And quietly running their establishments
Like upright citizens with a vote—
All standing beautiful and tall
To live and let live.

TUESDAY SERENADE

In the still moment
Before darkness and sleep, wind,
Having nowhere new to go,
Settles into the quietness
Of the old neighborhood.

Progress has no claim to this calm.
Lovers stroll past uselessly
Offering nothing for sale,
And boys gaze beyond cars
Lining streets with nowhere to go.

Here, in one small home,
A mirror whispers secrets to a face
Believing it becomes lovelier
As long smooth hair
Glides like water through a comb.

And there, on the porch,
In rhythm with a maple tree
A swing sways back and forth
On end-rhymed air.

WEDNESDAY CHERRY ROUNDS

Two squirrels are making their rounds
Around and around the cherry tree trunk.
While news spins and earth circles the sun
They play their hide-and-seek game.

Above it all a robin broods in her nest,
And bees are dizzied by blossoms going wild,
While from a telephone wire a crow looks down
On squirrels, robin, blossoms and bees.

When the crow takes flight to parts unknown
The tree stands tall, above the news,
And the bees, robin, and nest are stilled
By two squirrels hugging a cherry in bloom.

Thursday Hackberry Storm Services

The hackberries are silent and still again.
They performed their good works last night.

While winds screamed at the streets
And thunder dropped its black bombs,

I covered my head in the bed, afraid
The lightning was targeting me.

Like bent-over oldsters on canes in a park
The hackberries bowed to the storm

Without glancing down at the berries
They left behind like hail on the ground.

No one was charged a fee the next day
To see sparrows feasting on hackberry seeds,

Or thanked the trees that changed the storm's mind
And sent it howling right out of town.

GOOD FRIDAY TREE

(April 1, 1994)

Jesus speaks:

For once we have it my way:
My day—the bloody three hours
I'm deflowered every spring—
Double-featured with the agony
Of everyday April fool performances.

What a dreary day to try the public again
With my magic acts:
My walking-on-water routine,
My conversion of runoff to wine,
Or (in the Hollywood video style
Required of belief), my casting
Of terrible demons
Into unconscious streams.

Oh, if I could lure you close enough
To smell my flower,
My limbs would embrace you
With a simple truth:
That once upon a time
There were countless fools
Nameless like me, rooted,
Hung up on this or that,
Reaching for sky,
Unleaving

SATURDAY SWAMP OAK NEWS

Another big storm hit the city last night.
Nineteen swamp oaks that went wild in it
Are being charged with rioting.

Market profits today leaped to new highs
As investors took stock of the ratio
Of rising seas to the lower price of swamps.

Although loggers are busiest in spring
Economic indexes show the decline
Of oak forests holding up unsteadily.

And the Trucks won big over the Trees.
The away game begun decades ago
Quickly turned into a rout.

And to balance budgets politicians agree
Swamp oaks should be held accountable
For the riot of leaves littering the ground.

SUNDAY LOCUST FLOWER

In the meantime the honey locust,
Its heartwood steel-hard
And leaves more yellow than green,

Is the flower of a neighborhood
Lined with good citizens alive
In bedrooms, basements and brains

Where truth hides in the weeds
With loose thoughts and lusts,
And where little is known

And much is believed
Without troubling
The tree's dominance
Or dimming its radiance.

III

THE POETIC SCIENCE OF TREES

What [two teams of scientists] discovered was nothing less than a vast underground network, called...an arboreal Internet—christened the "wood wide web." Trees could actually communicate...in their own way, trees had feelings, they knew how to communicate with one another, and the strong were able to assist the weak.

    — Thomas Pakenham, *New York Review of Books*, 2016

Researchers say they've caught willow, poplar, alder, and birch trees listening to their own kind, and barley seeds listening to other barley seeds.

    — Sharman Russell, "Talking Plants," *Discover*, 2002

TREE

I love it tree because e love me too. E watching me same as you.

– Bill Neidjie, Gagudju elder, Australia

Bill's words—
Their simplicity, an intimacy
For what's beyond humanity.

Tree—so many words for thee
Booked, institutionalized, glossolalia
  Cooksonia
  Glassopteris
  Calamophyton primaevum
    Aesculus
    Betula
    Cercocarpus

Typed, like this or that, coned or not
    Coniferous, Deciduous
You not worker, poet, dancer, being

A product
    Apple and Apricot
    Banana and Breadfruit
    Cherry and Coconut
Your parts the whole of you
    Roots, limbs, leaves, bole

Invisible when used
    Lumber, flooring, cane and stool

No longer you
Your miracles and minds
By the grace of gods, a God and goddesses
Alive with earth, air, water, fire
He and She

In the park, across the road, on the lawn
    Aspen
    Basswood
    Chestnut
      and
    Yew

Tree also named *treow, trew, trow,* and *true*
How do we see through word-webs
So we may know
And speak to you?

Skin Deep Old Math

What does a plant remember? What is better to forget?
— Sara Laskow, "The Hidden Memories of Plants,"
Atlas Obscura, 2017

If bark is the tree's skin,
Like ours, holding tissues in,
How does it calculate by the hour
How much air to breathe in and out?

If in the stem or crown of a tree
We see no nerves or brain,
Where in heartwood is the mind
That rhymes the growth of rings
With the rhythms of sun and rain?

This story problem has untold terms:
Why did the tree first leaf out
Three days after an April freeze?
How did roots, branches and bole
Measure dawn and daylight degrees,

Memorize the number and duration
Of nights too cold, calibrate limb girth
To another season's wayward ways
So they accord with probability curves
Based on the wobbles of moon and earth?

No roots are squared during this calculus.
The tree stands silent and still for it,
Moved by the whirl of winds
While measuring by minutes and degrees
The hour for its leaves to unfurl.

MINDING THE OAK TREE SCENE

While Higgs fields are excited by invisible particles,
Minds, like boson masses, light little fires in the eyes
Of a girl with a toy broom, her grandparents, a cardinal,
And a tomcat stone-still on a lawn under a fat oak.

What was stirring the oak's leaves when the cat,
Poised still as death, tried to silence the atoms
Rushing insanely through cat heart, his eyes
Zeroed in on the cardinal serenading the scene?

The tomcat knows that the girl with the broom exists
Under the influence of oak leaves, but not why
Conscience stricken proteins cross synapses just in time
For her to scream the cardinal to safety into the tree.

And when the girl's grandfather looked up at the leaves,
Then bent a knee to tie the shoelace of the woman
He married a half-century ago, he saw his wife's face light up,
But not the waves and particles moving from her into him.

DEEP STATE

I go deaf, dumb and blind
Seeing a tree as silent, alone.

My senses, down to five,
Are too blurred to hear and see

Roots crackling messages
Electrically to bole and branch

From a hidden quilt
Of fungi dark-webbed with dirt.

How does leaf discern acrid from sweet
In the saliva of the worm eating it,

And how loud are the leaf alarms
Sent to wasp worm-eaters near the scene?

Who hears oak groves command oak patrols
To ward invading species away?

And why do birches care for Douglas firs,
Conspire with the mycelial underground

To feed conifers basking in birch leaf shade
The carbon milk the firs require to go on?

How can it be that a tree
Hears, feels, knows, cares

And prefers a dense forest neighborhood
To the high status of a busy boulevard?

I exhaust my days driving hours away
From mystery, my ignorance there bottomless,

The language whispers there unknown and strange,
Too slow and deep for me to see and hear
The groundwork clamor of quiet community.

TURFS

The gazelle flees and the king of beasts pursues
To make a cadaver of him, and to fill lion guts
With gazelle spirits morphing into lion flesh.

Lion rule is marked by piles of stench left behind,
His animal kingdom made emptier by hunger's excess.

Trees can't flee from lions, bugs, shade or gazelles,
Can't mobilize to invade a neighbor's back yard.

Their excrement is the banquet of leaves
Provided to the ground as blanketed feasts—lush,
Fragrant and moist humus that seeps into earth
To rise again, reborn, into plants lording over us.

Homebodies—trees have legs love-locked with dirt.
Roots don't run. They dig in, spread themselves thin,
Are deeply moved to expand their embrace
Of deep-state networks in the underworld.

They make allies of aliens in the undergrowth—
Enlist fungi filaments to work secretly for them,
Loop root strangers arm-in-arm, leg-over-leg
Into embraces that extend their ownership of forest floors.

From there the sap rises to show off the crowns
That cast shadows only hinting at the busywork below.

Meanwhile, in the upper air full of sun and wind,
Birds, beasts and bugs are made delirious

By arboreal flowers and fruit, their aromas and allures.

I routinely walk by without seeing
The wordless missionaries of sky and earth
Spreading the gospel of groves.

ACACIA SWEET-SOURS

Her many parts are well-used—
Her seeds for sauces, her tannins for dyes,
Her branches for fences, roofs and walls,
Her gum-sap for ointments and chewing gum,
Her oils for perfumes,
Her blossoms for liqueurs,
Her essences for mints, and Powerade.

In the biblical Book of Exodus
The timbers of her tabernacle
Resonated with many prayers.

She is well used but will not be abused
By a hungry gazelle on the prowl.
As her well-aged aromas spice the air
And the gazelle salivates
At the sight of her savory leaves,
She elevates her root chemistries
To new low-down heights.

She permits the gazelle to nibble her.
But suddenly her leaf juices—
Polyphenolic biomolecules
As astringent as sin—
Turn disgusting and foul.

Heart-burned, the gazelle turns up his nose
To find a fresher sister tree,
Downwind.

But the fresh sister tree, suddenly on alert,
Has received a whiff of warning
From the abused acacia. Her gassing
Tells the unnibbled sister
To go sour on the gazelle.

The confused gazelle,
With a lingering taste
Of sweet acacia on his lips,
Must hunger on and on,
Upwind.

OAK LOVELIFE

Full in the midst of his own strength he stands,
Stretching his brawny arms and leafy hands."
    – Virgil, *The Aneid*

The Roman poet got me all wrong:
I have brawny arms and leafy hands,

But those fluffy catkins, pollen gorged,
Have an ambiance entirely feminine.

Then check out the tiny leaf buds up high,
The flowers from my other brain, my crown.

I've got proof: I'm both staminate and pistillate.
At the slightest hint of wind I swing both ways.

I'm homebody too, king and queen renowned
For thousand year reigns in one small space.

A little fire under me can get me going—
Clear out the stubs and shrubs, the underlings,

Provide the breathing space I need
To give vent to the many ways I breed.

My delicate pollen has manly eyes.
It loves going everywhere, except the shade.

As male I'll fertilize every flower in my way,
And my blossom brides hug pollen from far away.

After my acorns, like penis heads, begin to swell,
They nose forest nooks to set their roots.

That keeps my tribe going on and on.
We're made this way. Please ask us why.

Then ask heaven and earth—
And the holy spirit of air—
Why we're so promiscuous.

WHAT AN ACORN KNOWS

There are more life forms in a handful of forest soil than
there are people on the planet.
   – Peter Wohllenben, *The Hidden Life of Trees*

How to grow down,
Suckle on dew,
Metabolize leaf litter
Gunk and grit—

How to instruct the memory
Encoded in heart pulp
By odd goddesses eons ago—
How to establish a claim, a shrine

Where root hairs remember
To feel their way
Into intimacy with loess
And world-wide web underground—

Where tendrils embrace the dirt
To perform mycorrhizal deeds
Naturally, mingling sweet mud
With moisture and fungal minerals—

In order to anchor a reign,
Tall, flowering, and strong,
A new lord of the rings
Directing a chorus of wind-harps
To hum clean airs.

ELM NAVES

Well before my leaves appear I, a queen
Of the order *Rosales*, the rose, am adorned
First by female flowers and then the male,
Both graced by pollens that fulfill spring air.

My male essences, eager to go out, ripen first,
Then surrender to the winds and take flight
To female flowers open to their touch.
There pale green seed clusters swell, hanging,

Ripening, and waiting for breezes
To carry them away to fields and forest floors.
There they descend to dig in and to inhale
The moistures and nutrients of my grand growth.

Minute by minute I ascend from dirt—stem swelling
Into trunk and limbs reaching for sky, arms rising
To form vast cathedral arches above human desires
Wandering in my shadows in boulevards and parks.

WANTON SILVER MAPLE WAYS

I'm even prouder and wilder with age—
When the shiny undersides of my leaves
Shimmer like jewelry in the hair
Of an old queen wanting to be seen.

I'm proud of my girth, my stature
Uplifted by limbs to a wide, round crown
From roots and hips wide enough
To provide nooks for squirrels to cozy in.

My roots have a yen for septic fields
Where drain pipes may sour my sap.
But I love going out and away.
Flowers and pollen—I live for them.

As grand old queen I put on display
My blossoms every spring.
The seasons seem careless and clued-in.
That's why we get along so infamously.

My flowers dizzy me with their diversity:
I permit them to be all female, or all male,
Or mostly female, or mostly male, or both.
They abide each other nicely. I have my ways.

Inside my perfect flowers male flowers may die.
Male clusters some females choose to ignore.
But my flower suites of single seeds, winged
As pairs, love to dally in wild orgies of air.

COTTONWOOD HIGHS

And what do people think of me when they,
Clueless about my private life, drive out of sight?
My heartwood is soft and white, theirs
Riddled with troubles, double-talk and noise.

Are my width and height too much for them?
I'm annoyed by their traffic and fumes,
And look down on any property claims
They make against my half-acre of sky.

I don't cry for help, or tell insects where to go,
Or enlist allies for some new war, or curse the wind
During storms gone wild, or make something wrong
Of bee sweet nothings on warm May days.

Nor do I bother to complain or respond
To somebody's blitz of opinions and beliefs.
My mind instead is tranquil, on high alert
For spring to release its blizzard of seeds.

Imagine two of us by a lake as woman and man—
Not touching as we stand in a warm blue sky
That drives us dizzy as we're under the spell
Of weavings fragrant with flowers and weeds.

That's when my catkins reveal themselves,
Let fly pollen the winds drizzle on my mate.
Then swelling begins until the catkins release
Their bridal shower of cottonwood snow.

That snow breezes over windshields and lawns,
And those seeds know enough to drift freely in air,
Find moist places to land and quietly settle in.
People go here and there. We dig in, grow up.

Aspen Communes

People call us quakers, but rarely socialists.
We flutter in cadence, and our bright bark
In its paper whites is too lovely for words.
We dance in unison on mountainsides.

We don't prefer old-fashioned simple sex
Climaxed by the success of a singular seed.
Our flowers know that wind-blown days
Lead to the embrace of limbs during silent nights.

The wind knows our seeds are scatterbrains,
That for them the moment must be just right,
That now and then the urge to merge succeeds
To bring one sapling babe from millions of seeds.

We prefer to be well-grounded, in the earth
Where roots crawl over each other like lovers
With skin moist, shiny, and smooth.
Our offspring pop out of those roots.

Clones, yes, why not? We tend to be beautiful,
And those born from rotting stumps fit in just fine.
You think our mating game is not hot enough?
A little brush fire now and then really turns us on.

Our leaf-dance performances show us off.
Our leaves are like little hearts, fluttering
Before they descend into the underworld to feed
Our vast society, linked leg-in-leg, arm-in-arm.

OLD NEWS

The tornado, with its twisted mind,
And the maniac hurricane,
And the volcano and tidal wave—
Their statements make the news
Loud and unclear

While old news carries on quietly—
Innuendoes, inflections, hums,
Tones vibrating invisibly
From the bellies of sap-sucking aphids
Silently swallowing ladybug larvae
While ants lick aphid backsides clean,
Their antennae stroking them,
Then colonizing them in leafy crowns
Where honeybees slurp the sap
And slip away to hives
Abuzz with ancient alchemies.

THE CARBON CYCLE: A Villanelle

We light our fires, make smoke of our despair.
We spew our troubles out and seldom say
The trees, dear trees, will give us back our air.

While busyness fills our minds with care,
Trees carry on in their ancient way,
To quietly make our skies more clear.

A tree takes our gassing deep inside its lair
Where it converts our waste through sweet decay
Into new leaves breathing out new air.

While cars and wars exhaust more lives with care,
The forest roots keep digging into clay.
We light our fires, make smoke of our despair.

While stem and branch do work we never hear.
Flowers and leaves return on time each May,
And trees, the trees, they give us back our air.

Their silent subtle work is more than fair.
They give more than they receive, it is their way.
We light our fires, make smoke of our despair
While trees, their lovely leaves, give us new air.

IV

THE TREE IN MYTH, LEGEND AND RELIGION

These woodland places
Once were the homes of local fauns and nymphs
Together with a race of men that came
From trunks, from hard oak...

 – Virgil, *The Aeneid*

We see also from the Book of Judges...that trees 'went forth on
a time to anoint a king over them; and they said unto the olive
tree, Reign thou over us.' When the olive tree refused, they went
to the fig tree with the same request...

 – E.A. Wallis Budge, *The Gods of the Egyptians*

And the Lord God planted a garden eastward of Eden; and
there he put the man whom he had formed. And out of the
ground made the Lord God to grow every tree that is pleasant
to the sight, and good for food; the tree of life also in the midst of
the garden, and the tree of knowledge of good and evil.

 – Genesis 2: 8-9

And the woman said unto the serpent, We may eat of the fruit
of the trees of the garden: But of the fruit of the tree which is in
the midst of the garden, God said, Ye shall not eat of it, neither
shall ye touch it, lest ye die. And the serpent said unto the
woman, Ye shall not surely die: For God doth know that in the
day ye eat thereof, then your eyes shall be opened, and ye shall be
as gods, knowing good and evil.

 – Genesis 3: 1-5

GREAT ROOTED BLOSSOMER

In the beginning She,
Primal Mother
The Sea, *madre* and *mare*, *mère* and *mer*,
Broke her waters, *vater* and *mutter*,
Over the continents
So life on Earth would be well governed
By her Primal Sister,
The Tree.

In old forests and new gardens
She increased and multiplied,
Her growth rooted like spreading words,
Her trunk a spine,
Her limbs and crown
Configuring the cross we are
Made of Heaven and Earth.

From her, Primal Sister, come honey and milks—
Apple, mango, date, plum, peach, apricot,
        lemon, fig and pear—
And hailstorms of seeds—acorns, olives, walnuts,
        pecans, chestnuts, macadamia, etc.—
Rained down, free.

All this from Her, alchemist witch
At once female and male, nurse and wife
Looming over holes and homes—
Primal Sister
Who stirs water, air, earth and light
Into her cauldron boles

While she is the instrument wind plays
To orchestrate the rhythms of blackbirds and days
With the rhymes of wildflowers and night.

She—who knows the serpent's embrace,
The ways of the underworld,
The wily commands of wrong and right—

Is named The World Tree
The Tree of All Seeds
The Soma Tree
The Tree of Enlightenment
The Tree of Knowledge
The Cross
The Tree of Life.

TREE TALK

They are said to speak to us
With voices that take us beyond ourselves:

To India, where in the rustling of leaves
The voices of gods and celestial nymphs
Are audible in the pipal tree.

To Crete, where the Selli tribe oracle
Hears the future foretold in winds
Answered by oaks that whisper and sigh.

To Dodona, the oak grove of Zeus
Where the oracle's words are aeolean.

To Alexander in Persia, worried
Because the male cypress, Mithra,
Tree of the Sun, tells him he'll lose,
And the female Mao, Tree of the Moon,
Informs his mother he'll soon be dead.

Or to China, where Master Zhuangzi
Conveys to busybodies the secrets of trees:
"I am myself, no other use to impose.
I am satisfied and big, and live to be old."

And to Dante's *Inferno*, black forest of the mind,
Gnarled and thorny, dense and desolate,
Where the voices of the damned, "serpents we,"
Once were men, "and each is now a tree."

Hell is where earth and heaven are apart:
Where a person is not also a plant,
Where Narcissus sees only himself in a pond.

And I—pathetic, fallacious—hear only myself
Speaking in terms I pretend to understand

When I am deaf to the silence of leaves
And to resonance in the rings of trees.

THE BODHI TREE

It is said that the original Bodhi Tree was planted in 288 BCE

After concentrating his gaze for six years on time
Long and short, and on all things in and out,
Up and down, here and there, nowhere and everywhere,
The Buddha made a pilgrimage to Bodh Gaya in India
And planted a fig tree there on a full-moon night.

Then the tree's mind became his, and his mind was the tree,
And the tree was and is him, and he is and was the tree.

As darkness dropped its centuries down
Demons from the hellfires of Hollywood
Opened their curtains to trouble him.
Monsters fired arrow and spear bombs,
Unleashed avalanches of fire,
And hurled boulders and mountains
At his mind—
While gorgeous Las Vegas card shark girls
Purred his name.

He saw flowers raining on him,
Translucent as rainbow lights.

His Bodhi Tree remained unmoved
As it moved and was moved around the globe—
From the Mahobodi Temple in India
To Ashoka's Kingdom and its jealous queen
Who tried to kill it with mandu thorns—
From there to Gaya in Ceylon, and then to Anuradhapura,
Across the sea to Honolulu, and then to Thousand Oaks,
California, U.S.A.

A few still see the Buddha tree there, also American,
Alive and still, serene, the way of being
Beyond suffering and happiness, equally tart and sweet,
More generous than trees of knowledge,
Their apples evil or good.

The Bodhi is here and there still,
Legs crossed like roots,
Trunk upright and poised,
Arms open to sky,
Limbs branching, bouquet of mind,
All leaves, flowers and fruit,
The fertility of the forever now
That is virtue, understanding, confidence,
Humility, and the acceptance that brings serenity.

GILGAMESH KILLS HUMBABA (Mesopotamia)

Humbaba, commanded by the gods to protect the sacred trees, never sleeps. He begs for mercy from Gilgamesh: 'I'll serve you as I served the gods. I'll build you houses from their sacred trees.'

From *The Epic of Gilgamesh, ca. 3000-2000 BCE*

Gilgamesh, in search of eternal life,
Has yet to see the worm crawl from the nose
Of Enkidu, his lover and friend,
And cannot foresee the Fall of Man
In the death of trees.

Terrified of the beauty and power they face,
Gilgamesh and Enkidu
Venture into a tangle of wood, branch and root.

In that forest they find Humbaba,
Monster protector of virgin groves
And servant of the gods of well-grounded life.

When Gilgamesh swings his ax
Into Humbaba's neck
His he-man demi-urge for present strife
Seeks jealous revenge
For what he can never have,
Eternal life.

The monster's fall cracks the earth in two.
The cedars, terrified, are slaughtered at his feet.

That night Humbaba's head,
Hanging from a tree,

Stares as it swings in dead air,
Wide-eyed as his cedar virgins
Are lugged away, one by one,
As slaves.

THE STAR IN THE COTTONWOOD TREE

*An adaptation of a traditional legend told by Mary Louise
Defender Wilson, "Gourd Woman," a Dakota elder born on
the Standing Rock Reservation in North Dakota.*

In the beginning, when everything was new,
The smallest was also the most curious star.
At night she was too small, and in the sun
No one saw her mind, the flickers of light,

Tiny and bright shining on animals and birds,
And no one heard her heart listening
To the music of village sounds, beautiful,
The flowers, grasses and worms,

And the people building their homes, gathering food,
The children laughing, old people chanting—
The work and play all musical.

I am too far away, she said, high in the sky.
I am heavenly and love the earth.
Can I, like a goddess or god, come down?
Is there a way I can be there and here?

And the winds said yes, you may descend
If you promise not to trouble the village life.

She came down to earth, to a cottonwood tree.
She lives now in that tree, swaying to the music
Of children and elders, their play and work.

And the people see how beautiful she is, her light,
Without seeing her face in the cottonwood tree.

THE RENEWAL OF DAPHNE

Ovid's *Metamorphoses, 8 CE*

Daphne, who ran from Apollo—
Faith-healer god of Delphi,
Failed lover of women,
Prophet and career pederast
Who preached the gospel "Know Thyself."

Daphne, one more woman
Who ran away terrified,
Because Apollo, her priest, abused
The better part of himself, the feminine
He saw in the faces of boys
And in the dreaded women
He saw as pythons, and killed.

Daphne ran because she refused to be raped.

She ran to the river, to her father Peneus,
Father of rivers, and surrendered herself
To life in the sacred waters there.
Virginal, she gave herself to the streams
That knew the secret ways to mother-sea.

The waters gently covered Daphne's feet,
And the purity of her powers
Took root in the riverbed.

As she let down her hair
Her limbs began reaching for sky.
From there she grew into a tree,
Elegant and beautiful.

From Daphne come forth bitter laurel leaves,
Woven into crown-wreaths for poets laureate.

PURIFICATION SCHEME

Myrrha, Venus and Adonis, from Ovid's *Metamorphoses*

What did the Magi understand about myrrh
When they brought its fragrance as a gift
To the Bethlehem manger scene, the new god
Born there destined to die and be reborn on a tree?

And what did they know about Venus' desires,
Or how the victim of a father's incestuous lust
And the poisonous jealousies of old gods
Can be reborn, purified by tree aromas and oils?

When Myrrha, still a girl, entered her old man's bed,
There beautiful Adonis was conceived,
And there Venus turned Myrrha into a lovely tree
Pregnant with the outcome of incest's lust.

As Adonis' moment to be born arrived, Myrrha's father,
Caesarean sword in hand, slashed open the tree,
And there Adonis, awash with milky perfumes,
Writhed his way through a knothole, and was born.

Venus, wonder woman of venom and venery,
Had a nose for the young boy, his god-like form
Too handsome to have a common birth
And yet untouched by her alchemy of desire.

Venus' lust for Adonis swelled as he grew,
Until the day she had her way with him.
Soon after their tryst he died, gored by a boar,
Finding peace at last in a virgin forest
Fragrant with the aroma of his mother's myrrh.

PENELOPE'S BED

Odysseus: "...the well-wrought bed. I worked on it, and nobody else. The long-leaved bush of a wild olive grew inside the yard flourishing in bloom. It was thick as a pillar is. So I built the bedroom round it till I finished it with close-fitted stones and roofed it well up above."

– Homer, *The Odyssey, XXIII*

She wept as she watched him undo the olive tree—
Behead its crown as he once took her maidenhead,
Then chop the stump, carve its outline with the ax,
Round the bedposts, straighten them with a line,
Drill an auger into them, then smooth the bed,
Adorn it with silver, ivory and gold,
Then lock in new ownership of the house
By constructing a chamber over the bed
Out of close-fitting stones that support the roof
        And closed her in.

For twenty years Penelope had ruled her own house
As matriarch, fidelity to her and her powers
Conferred by ancient precedent.
She governed the economies of labor and food,
And kept her selfish suitors at bay.

Her husband's hero-parade required her retreat.
In exchange for his wins on the road,
The spoils of his loins and sword,
She surrendered the concord of the loom.
And when he lured her into his olive tree bed
She trusted its artwork to cover for his artifice.

She understood the hard grounds
On which her new household was debased—
Not grains aroused by rains and soil
But gains stolen by armor and sword.

In her new olive tree bed she began to sleep
With her man's victories, and his long absences—
His flirtations with Nausicaa and her maids,
His swine lolls with Circe, and siring of a son, Teleganos,
That sent him scurrying to his seven year Calypso fling.

With the aroma of the wood dizzying his brain,
The clever hero laid Penelope in his new olive bed.
But he, who usurped her long rule, could not see
His years gaining on him, or himself again
On a distant crossroad, like Oedipus,
This time cut down—by Teleganos—stranger furious
At the odious Odysseus, himself a stranger
To the hero-husband who sired a son and fled
From bastard Teleganos,
Who got a woman's revenge on him
That left no scent of olive on the bloody road.

The Golden Bough: Two Views (Ancient Rome)

1. Aeneas Founds an Empire: Rome

The hate called heroism still lingers
In the air above a Troy no longer here.
How do we remake evils some still revere?

Aeneas makes a clean escape from the fires of Troy
To make his fortune in clear Italian air.
By what authority does a loser win a new life?

The Sybil, Deiphobe, seven hundred year old hag—
Younger than the laurels above Apollo's temple—
Knows the underworld way, the way of trees.

"Will you come," she asks, "with me to the Stygian river,
The river of death leading to the oak with the Golden Bough
That stands before the gate of the Underworld, the way in?"

He needs female advice and guidance—from Venus,
Venerable sister-goddess of venom, venery and vines,
And chaste Diana, queen of moon periods and forest
    witcheries.

"My two doves," Venus says, "will lead you to the old oak.
There you will lop off the Golden Bough, but carefully,
Reverently, so a new limb will grow in its place."

His Golden Bough, passport to the Underworld, he gifts
To Proserpina, Queen of seeds and roots, as he enters
The land of the living dead and hidden life of trees.

He crosses the river of death, its three-headed dog,
And passes the three-walled prison full of sufferers.
Beyond this gnarl of woe he sees the Elysian fields,

Where the pleasures of pastures and peace cross his legacy
Yet to be born—the Caesars—the future of Rome
Grounded not on fertile fields but monuments and war.

By way of the Golden Bough the way of patriarchs is
    authorized,
The lovely branch weaponized as scepter useful to the
    business
Of empire and war, in palaces stone-deaf to the way of trees.

2. Diana: The Pruning of Priests

Diana's devotees tell a different tale.
This goddess, virginal, remains untouched
In forests alive with her pristine fertilities.

As priestess of sacred oaks she performs
The periodic ritual that maintains, reasons
And rounds the authority of slave and priest.

By her command a slave is required
To cut the Golden Bough from the sacred oak,
And to kill its priest, lord of the tree.

In this way the slave becomes a new priest
Who rules until a new slave arrives to harvest
A renewed Golden Bough—and prune the old lord.
Brought down by the just symmetry of forest ways,
Priests become slaves, and slaves are reborn as priests.

Thus Diana, Queen of Forests, orchestrates
Earth's line of succession as a round of low and high,
With new life and freedom ascending from old growth.

POSTSCRIPTURE TO GENESIS: A SONNET

Wild winds have stripped bare the apple tree,
Have made rotten wastrels of her lush excess
On ground subversive worms routinely bless
As windfall for a late autumn feeding spree.

When the lovely apple in Eve's sly eye
Decomposes with the beauty of the fall
And makes her the goat who damned us all,
With what revenge scheme did she comply?

To what plot did an approving God subscribe
When His snake took Eve and laid her low?
Those co-conspirators of all our woe
Both knew she'd fall hard for the apple bribe.

As bachelor Satan-Lords of the Tree of Life
Neither had good use for earth or wife.

THE LEASE OF NATURE

Third Apparition:
  Macbeth shall never vanquish'd be until
  Great Birnam wood to high Dunsinane hill
  Shall come against him.
Macbeth:
  That will never be.
  Who can impress the forest, bid the tree
  Unfix his earth-bound root?

  – Shakespeare, *Macbeth, IV*

When Macbeth honed his schemes
On the steel-edged teeth of a brain
Stewing the weird alchemies
That turn water and milk into blood—
Conscience seeped into the underworld
Where roots perform the best practices
Of the four elements.

Can heartwood remain untouched,
Unmoved by human wrongs?

When noise and war have no feel
For the whisperings of roots and leaves,
Or for forests as landlords with natural rights
Lending their spaces and powers to us—

And when trees are also citizens taxed to death
By mercenaries, war machines and malls,

Can forests remain untouched, unmoved?

Listen up, Macbeths! Quiet armies have their ways!

The forest has a webwork of family ties,
A guerrilla army allied to sky and earth,
A silent majority with underground cells.

Jesus And His Tree

He loved mornings best,
The hint of dew on grass,
The air-brushed shadows on sand,
And light translucent on leaves.

Bent over, his robe spread wide,
His ear to the ground,
He listened for the sea,
Then he arose
To measure the hunger,
The incessant pull in the heart
Of the wood, from roots,
Their white tendrils curled.

Above, visible against sky's sea-blue,
The pendulous figs fell at his touch.
Well he knew the feel
Of their unshaved skin,
The globed weight in his palms,
Their slippery taste,
The sandy grit of their seeds.

"I am the vine," he whispered,
As his fingers caressed the tree.
Feeling for the fragrance in its core
He ascended to display
Its antlered canopy to the sun.

DOGWOOD MIND

According to legend Jesus died on a dogwood tree cross. Dogwood blossoms are said to reveal the scars of Jesus' crucifixion, the edges of their petals blood-stained, their center a crown of thorns.

The dogwood memorizes the seasons by heart,
Wisely knows which months wait winter out.
It has a feel for the sun's March tomfooleries
Designed to debauch tulips asleep in their beds.

It has no memory of the Long March,
Gulags, or concentration camps,
No recollection of names in the news.
But in a mind busy with blossoming
It adorns itself yearly to mark the death
Executed on wood centuries ago,
On a hill far away.

OUR LADY OF THE FIRE

Notre Dame Cathedral, Paris 2018

Awe goes up in smoke
As "The Forest" attic—
The hand-hewn lattice work
Shaped from fifty-two acres
Of ancient oak—
Collapses with the spire
Of Notre Dame Cathedral.

Beyond belief the holiest of shrines
For believers and art devotees
Is deconstructed by degrees

As *puros*, purifying fire,
Breezes smoke to the woodlets
Outside the City of Light.

There leaves shudder
And roots claw more deeply in

Reciting by rote: from wood fires
New forests arise.

What did the woodmen see
Eight hundred years ago
When the trees, the giant oaks—
Silent, holding their ground—
Were hacked down and hauled
Like wagon loads of slaves
To serve priests and kings
Eager to brew their stew

Of magic and art
To achieve the transubstantiation
Of Christ's body and blood
Into the Virgin Mary's stone walls?

Did "The Forest" timbers,
The cathedral's crown of thorns,
Remember the way of woods?

How from wood fires
New forests arise.

What imp, above or below,
What rebel impulse
Alive in tired worker
Or careless priest,
What electrical impulse,
Natural philosopher and historian,
Sparked the first flame?

And what monument will be recomposed
From the ashes of the Virgin Queen?
Will she, white-washed
Aphrodite, Demeter, and Artemis,
Reappear as New Woman
Staring sad-eyed at tourists
While space-age overlords
Build their new empires?

What reforestation
Of desire, kindness and belief
Will arise from her blackened bones?

Holy Day Trees: A Carol

When birds cry and wild winds scream
Because ice has whitened the winter sun,

What do forests breathe into air
For a mother cradling a new-born son?

When solstice stars, distant and dim,
Are lost in black oceans of space,

How can arms radiate enough care
For the small face huddled there?

When the blitz buries the corn on the plain
And we cower against the cold blowing in,

Why does a mother wake from her sleep
To offer her breasts to a child?

On frozen nights when pines are undone
And limbs shivered by winds going wild,

Well-seasoned trees know deeply by heart
The old music toned in their woods,

The hymns hummed by summer and spring
Deepened by chords the storm winds sing.

IN THE PALM GROVE

In the palm grove
Where lion and jackal lie low,
Hunger springs of necessity
But neither curses its foe.

When serpent and dove
Eye each other in the same tree,
Wonder and guile lift their heads
Without hate or love.

In churches where Christians
Make war from hymns,
Confusion and belief sing
Like ghosts to angel hosts.

Where hippo and gazelle
Drink from the same pond
Shaded by the same palm grove,
There is no holy war.

V

DECLINE AND FALL

What do you call it, whatever it is, when forces of wilderness and weather, of animal kingdoms and plant life, have been so transformed by human activity they are no longer truly 'natural'?

– David Wallace-Wells, *The Uninhabitable Earth: Life after Warming*

EARTH WARMING: An Allegory

Before rains began melting the glacial seas
Her citizens drifted south to cityscapes
Crossed by freeways, railroads and wires.

There she was stirred by the alchemies
That made her high, and spaced her out
Into the netherlands of jet-streamed sky.

Soon her flesh and bones went digital
Over villages at war with secret codes
Encrypted by the high priests of memory banks.

From there she looked past factory smoke
At the wreckage of self-driven cars,
Assembly-lined and newly microchipped.

When rain brought floods she felt new warmth
Rising toward her old heart-level depths.
In her belly she felt the sea's undertows.

The rising waters began composing her.
As her body heat warmed sand and sky
Rains fell like hair over islands sliding into sea.

I'm going south, she declared as tempers flared.
She wore mud-caked boots as she plodded
Past armies of great plain fields, uniformed.

She paused when she saw the moon,
Full and almond white, nested

In the horned branches of an apple tree

Presiding over a serpent embracing it,
Lord of the tree's unforbidden fruit
Scattered on the ground, as usual.

ANTHROPOCENE

Achieved. Evolved. Destined.
I think, therefore I think
Sequence, causation and purpose
Are the same.

Therefore the death of dinosaurs,
Caused the asteroid to propose
The death of dinosaurs, the finale
Of every last one of their fat tails,
So I, achieved, evolved, destined
Could make my own way
By cunning savage and sly,
Tail-less

In a new world, because I think
I think I am destined to be
Unconfused
By trumped up towers
Above marshy swamps,
Not-me the unholy mess
Mineral carbon oxygen,
Vegetable buckthorn spiny,
Animal raccoon and buzzard—
Not-me.

And rattlesnakes not me,
With those tails.

And trees not me,
Things uncrowned by priests,

Their rootwork unsalaried,
Their veins slurping muck,
Their leaves falling off and down,
Messing with lawns, in constant need
Of trims,
With nothing to say to me,
Anthropos,
Man and (woman)
Tail-less lord of the flies,
Proprietor of pulpwood,
And lord of its rings.

SPRUNG FEVER

Two months before the first day of spring
A blizzard of blossoms drifted down dead

From trees aglow with drunk bees dancing
June-like wedding toasts from bride to bride.

Robins circled deliriously in January skies,
The polar winds there so hot and cold

They left us shivering with those sharp chills
Nasty flirts exude as they cheat past.

And the apple, apricot, cherry and pear
Were brilliant again, so suddenly in bloom

They inspired teenage girls to hum canticles
While dancing rock and roll topless in church.

All this while groundhogs, terrified by tremors
Of distant glacial moves, dug more deeply in.

That January blossom blizzard is plural proof:
A brave new world unseasoned by ancient turns

Has new laws of nature in store for family trees:
June marriages made in frozen Minnesota skies

With hot blizzards of shower gifts not far behind,
Frigid wedding cake icings to top things off,

Flowers raining down on rainbow slicks of oil,
And other bizarre beauties never seen before.

POLICY

The news is saying yes,
Money, not leaves, will be raked in.
This free-for-all is decreed
By the Ministry of Mouthing.

This new law of nature requires
Paper loads to be employed
To leverage walls, rivers,
Walled in streets, and banks.

The paper will not be edible.

Nor will flowers dying in beds
Be insured against viral abuse,
The miscalculations of rising seas,
And the ghosts of barren trees.

AFTER THE LOGGING

Jus primae noctis (or Droit de Seigneur): The law that gave a feudal nobleman the right to have sex with an indentured bride on her wedding night.

The carnage is cold-blooded white,
The winter work of a sharp lord
And his chain-sawing hired hacks
Lopping off limbs, slicing trunks
And making railroad ties from oaks.

In full daylight the lumber lord
Exercises his *jus primae noctis.*
He loves to see them in rows,
Still and naked on bare hillsides,
And has no ear for their silences
Or for the fresh scents they bleed
Into air, or why the blanket of snow
Tells him it's time to get rid of his wife.

Pulp Fiction

The limbs shudder in poplar groves.
The chainsaws there have sharp appetites

For the pretty ones destined for sale
In the slave market of romance and chills.

Saws leer as they eye one up and down,
Revving up their hunger for tender ones.

A schoolgirl, leaning away, is next,
She is slender, smooth, untouched,

Perfect for the slurry of stories potboiled
To rise to the top of best-seller lists.

The paper trail leads from the forest
To the factories of crime and romance,

From there to a window's seductive leer felt
While her man downstairs watches TV, pulped.

In the carte blanch between the lines
She is too scared to scream or speak,

Her legs too frozen to run and hide.
The men will not let her leave.

NEW YEAR DAZE

As citizens count down
The passing new year hours,
Father Time hides, shivering
With aspens in the dark.

The crowds in New York
And Washington, empirical,
Are awed and amused
As night skies are fireworked,

And good old boys see no hag
Hanging around, with an eye
To harvest the genitals
Of royal bearded lords.

Only ancient oaks have a feel
For the scythe Time hides
In its shroud, steel hot to slice flesh
From the backbones and arms

Of careless sons who ooh and ahh
The display, and curse the sub-zeroes
And snows that hardened the bones
Of the cherry trees they rode as boys.

PHANTOM PAIN

She goes everywhere in search of his leg—
In back streets and warehouse schools
That have no memory of wronging
The pasture or barn, or her man

Who once upon a time stood safely on base
In a field of dreams, gazing in wonder
At wind-blown trees in azure skies,
As another new war went on and on.

He now litters the ground in a faraway city
With leftover bodies and bullet-riddled walls.

All night the dogs of war keep nosing her
For the scent of her new wedding sheets.
She, flesh of his flesh, keeps feeling
His leg over her, AWOL from her bed.

She first felt the presence in October air
As a cold-blooded attack on her spine
By fall's turncoat leaves dropping from trees,
Their limbs already frigid and bare.

SUMMER STORM

When we heard the news—
El Nino was coming soon—we hid
With a candle and canned goods
In the basement of the soul.

With our ears to the ground
We heard the Valkyrie trains
Screaming in tune with the prayers
Believers performed during their exodus.

That night all the trees,
The wonderful trees,
Obedient to wind's ways, fell.
They fell across streets and railroad tracks.

Nobody could progress.
The trees missed every cottage, barn
And beaver dam, the wonderful trees
That made the trains run late.

WAKE WINDOW

The window is wide enough
To show the smiling faces

Of the petunia choir on display
In the planter on the sill.

There too it provides a nice view
Of lawn all-green, weed-free.

A sparrow on a telephone wire
Feels small talk tingle its claws

As lines of cars stop on red
Before crawling downtown.

In that window the sky is too grey
To have a say about the odorous

Funeral flowers in bouquets,
Or about the winds streaming

Silently through branches of trees
That sway, dancing air on its way.

Where are they going, these winds
That blow through trees looking down

On traffic not carried away
To forests and fields open and free?

TIDAL WAVE

He loses standing when the wave
Sweeps parking lots into the sea
With the junk of wires and TVs
Fashioned from ores
Natives dug out of Congo holes
While suckling their babes on mud.

He rides the wave like a boy
As it peels the concrete back
And the water's tongues
Lick the bodies of cars,
The crankcases, batteries and grilles,
The smooth hoods and trunks
Swirling toward sinkholes
And rainbow rills of oil
Shimmering on the sunny sea.

He lets everything go
The way of the tidal wave—
Clocks, cell phones and radios,
The years spent waiting at traffic stops,
The dirty little wars in exhausted air
Whitewashed

By winds blowing casinos down
Into seaside undertows
Until the progress of events
Turns him toward a cow on a hill

Standing alone
Under a full moon
Next to a huddle of trees
Still hanging on.

At His Mother's Burial

When the preacher proclaimed
"Ashes to ashes" over the burial hole,
He lowered his head in prayer
To let the reformation begin.

In riverbeds thought ran dry,
Emptying into a pit
Where earth, air, water and fire
Hiss at everlasting life,

And dust settles on prairie grass
Shadowed by the murmuration
Of starlings weaving melodies
In a symphonic search for new nests.

He stared into the vacancy
To see the woman who created him
Unconditionally. Eyes were closed
And words silenced in air

Humming with scents of decay,
The work of blood-water and tears
Already at work in soil's ooze
To recompose from ash of flesh

New tendrils and roots, stem and bole,
New saplings able to weave and dance
As terrible storms pass through.

VI

THE GIVING TREE

There they go.
Look at those dogs go!
Why are they going fast
  in those cars?
What are they going to do?
Where are those dogs going?
Look where they are going.
They are all going to that
  big tree over there.

    – P.D. Eastman, *Go, Dog, Go!*

Why are trees such social beings? Why do they share food with
their own species and sometimes even go so far as to nourish
their competitors? The reasons are the same as for human
communities: there are advantages to working together. A tree
is not a forest. On its own, a tree cannot establish a consistent
local climate....If every tree were looking out only for itself, then
quite of few of them would never reach old age.

    – Peter Wohlleben, *The Hidden Life of Trees*

Once there was a tree...and she loved a little boy....But as the
boy grew older he began to want more from the tree, and the tree
gave and gave....
    – Shel Silverstein, *The Giving Tree*

TREE LUST

When young he had no mind for trees—
The dying ones, Dutch-Elm diseased
With beetle hieroglyphs inside the bark,

And dead ones bald as worm-eaten men
Enduring the sullen grind of insect hours,
Their skin worn rough by careless winds—

Or fallen ones, their wreckage in a ditch
Overrun by armies of termites and ants
Silently turning white bones to dust.

Now, after he has them cut and stacked,
Gathered in his arms and carried to the hearth
Where their embers pulse like hearts on fire,

He can't turn away from a wintering one,
Her autumn dress fallen at her feet,
Her limbs reaching for sky,
Her form naked and open, inviting him.

WINDFALL

Scattered on a busy boulevard lawn
The fallen apples blush and shine
As they wait to be chosen and held,

No questions asked about ownership,
Or about how seeds morph into fruit
Unfurled from soil's netherlands.

Apples—rained on the grass from above
From blooms flowered like wedding gowns
In the fragrance of evenings and dawns.

Free—the work of bees delirious with desire
For buds swollen into unforbidden fruit
Delicious, hanging on for dear life

Until a breeze sends them forth quietly
Down onto the lawn next to the street
Nobody owns, the faces in passing cars

Fixed on tail lights not bright enough
To shine on one soul thankful enough
To see the gift, stop, gather and feast.

TREE HOUSE

After the preacher took a deep breath
And his word-load disappeared in a mirror,
The front window opened itself wide
And the trees welcomed themselves in.

When the cat caught the fragrance of roots
She purred and made a pillow of her paws,
Then watched starlings enter their glide
Of shadows on wallpapered walls.

His daughters came in with the trees,
Girls decked out in branches and leaves,
And the grand-dame also appeared, the witch
Who smiled as she watched and wove.

Open windows, the old crone sang,
Open them all, air everything in.
Let all the trees into the house.
Let there be swaying, good air, and light.

All clocks suddenly told the same time,
And earth kept wobbling with sun and moon,
And trees achieved residence in the living room.

Nursing Home

A gnarled willow, haunches spread wide,
Spreads her limbs over a ruined house

On a sidestreet where traffic noise
Grays the weeds crowding in on it.

It's a shaken shack, like an old man
Crippled, homeless, and alone,

Its windows eye-patched, boarded up,
Its rafters bowed, weighing on its mind.

Huddled within the willow's limbs
The old house squats in the shade

As a pigeon in the willow tree gazes,
Stoic and calm, as if keeping watch.

On Saying Farewell

(To my sister Aurora)

As she stood on the lawn
And watched me leave,
The pallor on her face
Dimmed the colors of dawn.

When I waved farewell
Two cars passed on the street.
In one a bald man drew a blank.
The other sent me a hanging grin.

I didn't think to ask their names,
And then they were gone,
Wherever everyone goes.

But then I saw Aurora's chestnut tree
Standing so beautifully in the way.
The dark green of its leaves

Hovering over a girl in a pink dress
Skipping her way from school to old age
Inside the shades of widespread limbs.

How to Turn the Other Cheek

1.
Stiffen your jaw
Against the latest bomb blast of sun-baked belief.
Let its words shatter against hard bone.
Take deep breaths to let blowback gather strength.
Hide your spit beneath your tongue.

2.
Lay yourself down in the lap of desire.
Let your mind lose itself in its fragrant folds
Until you close your eyes and sleep comes.

3.
Surrender jowl and jugular
Unconditionally to the fanged beast.
Relax when it sinks teeth in you.
Imagine yourself as virginal.
In the spiked thrill finally achieved
Gaze wide-eyed at the calm pond,
The delirium of warmth draining down.

4.
Be a leaf
That rights itself
As winds blow away.

LIVING OUTSIDE-IN

Truck and bus diesel dizzies him.
When he noses his way along streets
The stench of battlefield corpses seeps
Into naves through cracks in stained glass.

Daily a new woman appears at his door.
The lines on her face are familiar and strange.
She desires to make love anytime, anywhere,
Then writes her name on his mirror and leaves.

The random intrudes on his schemes,
The egret on one leg in a backwater swamp
Shimmering in the bad air of jet fuel blues
While atoms and galaxies dance on, unseen.

He sits still long enough to see one leaf
And one stone happening on the grass.
He makes eye contact with one face in a crowd.
He finds the stone in the face, the face in the leaf.

Advice To A Boy

The cottonwood, her branches
Like vast wings spread
Over a brooding teenager's woes,
Whispers the obvious:

Look up,
And I will take you up
And away with me.

Look up,
Beyond the thick wrinkles of my skin,
How I just am
Alive in sun or rain,

Just hanging on,
Just hanging out,
And, quite naturally,
Feeling high.

TRAINING THEM

When he tried to explain to his kids
(in the middle of the night).
What it was like to be
On another runaway train

Speeding down the tracks
To some place all wrong for them
(he'd paid their fares, up front),
How he was certain, maybe,

They too would soon wish
They were somewhere else, anywhere,
Maybe back in the same old house
(he'd gladly pay their way home, again)

Where he was now—
The best he could do is resolve
To slow the ride by asking them,
Please, to sit still near to him

For a minute or two or three
(they owed him one)
Alone in the caboose, with their backs
To the engines going wild,

So they could more clearly discern
Where they had come from
(They seldom ask) and therefore
Where they are going,

And never (like him) lose count
Of the tick-tock clatter of cross-ties
Speeding away into white-noised years
(where have they gone?),

On the parallax of rails
That converge to a dot
In a landscape of flowers,
Ponds and trees
(So beautiful).

New Year Blessings

When the holiday wrapped its mind around
The fact the shades indeed had fallen
Over the neighbor boy's teenage eyes,

We huddled against the bone-white cold,
Survivors of this out of the blue cheap-shot
That rattled snake-eyes up and down our spines.

I paused to review the renewals of age:
Our children safely gone forth, charged
To try their wings above sinking coastal lines,

And our new freedom from performance stunts
In disheveled beds, the clarity of loose thoughts
About the blurry lines between desire and love.

My love ignores the floor I somewhat swept,
And pots somewhat scrubbed, dishes still stacked.
She is deeply in love with another good book.

And the New Year sun still shines on white birch,
And on the rainbow hues of blackbird wings
Shimmering above tree shadows cast on snow.

PEAR LOVE

Just before he snaps a stem like a neck,
The limb resists the letting go
And makes a garden thief of him, an Adam
With no knowledge of evil or good.

The deluge comes soon afterward,
A downpour too much for bushels and bags.
I am too much for you, they whisper
As he keeps reaching for them in his sleep.

The pears keep descending like leaves,
Scattered like tsunami debris left behind,
Or like refugees fleeing air raids in Syria,
Wondering why they're so small on this earth.

Suddenly branches seem bare, undone,
Tree purpose achieved, leaving
The heavy load of work ahead too much
For him alone, in years too few.

Then the day after the first October frost
Sends a blitz through his bones, he looks up,
Sees one alone, like the woman he loves
Still hanging on, poised to fulfill the fall.

AEOLIANS

I, times you, my love,
We are *The* Life, definite article,
Singular noun and verb
Moved by the unseen—
The way
Branches and leaves permit
Airs to pass through

For the rivers and streams
To carry on with storms,
Wildfires and dreams
Making their rounds—

As if we together
Are branches and leaves
Waving wands
To conduct the music
The trees compose.

SPRING CLEANING

When the time has come to clarify—
Toss out the old bike, the hose with the hole,
The stinky hats and shoes, fish tank, stale paint,

The attic stuff, cracked violin, boxfuls of loose thoughts
On paper scraps, First Communion and wedding suits,

And, if he dares, the browned photos
Of unremembered faces and names—

It's time to ask earth what he owes
For freeloading here, his paying no rent

To the lordly valleys deserts forests seas
And spacious sky Grand Canyon depths
Landfilled by the messes he makes.

The time has come to clarify what gift
He can provide from this body
Exuding odors, phew!

So it may rise again, perhaps

Suspended in a naked cottonwood, alone
And beautiful on a snow-frozen plain

Where rainbows shimmer
Off the wings of the blackest birds

That loft themselves into winds
Whistling weird music through white bones.

VII

BURYING THE TREE

There is something permanent about the picture of my father by the old fig tree in our suburban Detroit back yard. I see him loitering around the tree's hem, as if his presence will coax favors from this mistress long-accustomed to fulfilling her promise in good slow time. On blue late summer days he offers a handful of figs all around, a smile on his face as he opens one with his thumbs for everyone to see inside. All the work he did in the yard—from saving old boards in the shed to staking tomato plants with strips of rags—resolves itself into the image of him next to that tree. It's an old black and white photo I carry in my mind—one strangely suffused with the early-evening colors of summer fields and blossoming things.

A fig tree in a suburban Detroit back yard—so out of place. Like Frost's peach tree trying to survive a winter storm in Vermont.

We think of the tree. If it never again has leaves,
We'll know, we say, that this was the night it died.

Detroit's winter storms are enough to do a fig tree in, especially since all trees there contend with elements manufactured into urban blight.

No one knows for sure how the first fig tree arrived. Peasants from southern Italy who came to American shores a century ago smuggled a few sprigs in with their other goods. Imagine what went into those leathery suitcases as weather-worn as the people who lugged them off the boats: The suit he was married in and her wedding dress; the pillowcases she herself embroidered on long winter nights; a few special dishes inside towels and underwear; a pot and pan; birth certificates and old deeds; browned photos of members of the family, the piazza, the goat left behind; and thick slices of dried hard bread wrapped in a linen cloth. Essentials. Among them, carefully bedded inside a sheet or the arm of an old wool coat, a green-stemmed branch of the fig tree still standing next to a road leading from and to a town.

The sprig endured the Ellis Island lines, gave customs the slip, ended up on a train heading to New Jersey or Boston or Pittsburgh or Detroit, surviving on its own green sap until one day rough hands dug a small hole and gave it a place in American soil.

By the time my father abandoned Detroit for a retirement house in Florida, his tree had grown to over twenty feet. Its origins are obscure, the name of its Old World home and original smuggler lost to memory. But as it grew it established the legitimacy of its family line, becoming the stem for other branches of a community bonded more by language than by blood or place. "This is Don Vincenzo's tree," I see my father saying to me. "It's from your uncle Tony Posa's tree, the little one in back, and he got his from Pasquale Bruno, who got his right from Don Vincenzo's tree." Though Pasquale was not related to Don Vincenzo, and though Don Vincenzo was long dead and gone, the old Don's tree, once named, held sway. On August evenings when the men gathered in each other's yards to feast on wine and talk in the language they never left behind, the figs they tasted were all from Don Vincenzo's fabled tree. And when it was time for newcomers to be cut in, it was somebody's version of Don Vincenzo's tree that was broken off and offered around like pieces of bread to strangers on trains.

The poet Frost, perhaps because he felt the cold not only in his name but in his bones, understood the fig tree problem well:

What comes over a man, is it soul or mind—
That to no limits and bounds he can stay confined?
You would say his ambition was to extend the reach

110

Clear to the Arctic of every living thing.
Why is his nature so hard to teach
That though there is no fixed line between wrong and right,
There are roughly zones whose laws must be obeyed?

The fig tree in Detroit was not merely displaced; it was, like its devotees, out of place. Most of the immigrants from southern Italy who came to America did not abandon a nascent nation-state called Italy existing mainly in the minds and bureaucracies of liberal reformers from cities in the north; they left behind the Old Country, an impoverished but ancient way of life defined by the climate and landscape of their Mediterranean regions. The Old World tax collector often took what he could get—a cheese, chicken, goat, or promise—from peasants who mined the soil for their only currency, the earth's vegetables, grains, and fruits. When American trains took these peasants further west and north, mainly to factory work in cities frozen a good part of the year, they found themselves increasingly out of touch with warm skies and the rough dry soil that had to be coaxed into providing them the stuff of life.

Many, including my father, threatened to return to the Old Country for good, their debates, often articulate and hot, lasting into the night. America yes, but America no. Yes, there was work, a necessity, and there was money, a luxury, here too. Indoor plumbing, a washing machine, and maybe someday a car. Who would ever have these things over there?

But something was lacking here.

How to find words, the right word? Respect. Men who never went to church required respect for some sort of God, for just and often unwritten laws, for learning, for the authority of parents and the innocence of girls.

And so much taste had been lost. The fruits and vegetables in the stores were never fresh enough; the meat had a strange stink; and the water never turned into wine quite as clear and fragrant as the wine back home. A few returned to the Old Country for good, others to visit villages, aging parents, wives left behind. But most, not quite mindful of how way leads on to way, found themselves on ever-widening American highways inexorably leading them further from each other too.

Confronted by a Great Plain opening itself to the leveling of identity, the new arrivals tried to regroup along Old Country lines. In cities Italian neighborhoods formed, the groceries and delis dense with imported aromas and tastes. In homes the old rules still held: Papas, absent in their work, pretended to their habits of command, while Mamas, lost indoors most of the time, made the decisions and all the beds and bread. On Saturday nights everyone went to the wedding at the Italian-American hall, and as midnight neared even the old people who sat sad-faced watching the dance leaped up to do the *tarantella* one more time. Late October was sausage-making time, many old hands cranking away at the handle of some uncle's meat grinder; that was also when a delegation went to the railroad yards to check out the California grapes. All was momentarily right with the world when the fragrance of newly fermenting wine filled the house.

But these were a people—most of them—who for centuries had made a living off the land. What they understood best was the struggle—and habits—of small growing things. For them the weather was more than the stuff of small talk, medium of social relationship; it was vital friend or foe. The earth's temperament was craggy and dry, its good humors dragged out of it with a hoe. It was a terrible shame to waste anything, for everything had some use. The ground had the strange power to purify, turn manure into tomatoes and beans. Life was not merely life but *La vita*, the word's definite article at once drawing attention to life's finite singularity and to a special wholeness deserving a proper name. For the peasant the hours were full of toil, survival dependent on sky's balanced relationship with soil. There had to be moments when men and women stood back from their work in awe of the incomprehensible beauty of their terrible world. Yes, despite the priests, God did exist, somewhere out there in the landscape, his rule as arbitrarily mysterious as some monarch or dictator presiding in a distant Rome, but sacred because ultimately good. And Evil was out there too—omnivorous, persistently crowding in on the small good things, its craving for more than its lush share wasteful and unbalanced. Like weeds. Therefore those who wronged the group had to be taken in hand personally, and pulled out by the hair.

My father was like many of them—a peasant farmer and stone mason whose New World work took him into the coke ovens and open hearth of the Ford Rouge plant. Plant and hearth indeed, this massive and bizarre configuration of sheds, smokestacks, and pulleys that took earth's elements in and subjected them to a series of alchemical processes resulting in miles worth of cars and mountains of waste. Black-faced from the smoke and grime, my father spent many a dark day—thirty-three years, a Christ's age—doing his part to translate the ore from the Minnesota iron ranges into the gold that never materialized as he waited in line to be handed his paycheck every week. Prosperity followed unnaturally enough.

After working the fires of the coke ovens and open hearth he went home to Old Country work. Somebody's brick or stonework needed repair—the work of hands and ancient chemistries. In the small garden in back the grapevines went up with the trellises that walled the yard in green, as if to enclose the tomatoes, peppers, and eggplants into a world of their own.

But the little New World garden was inevitably done in by the cold. *Terra maligna*—the sky too perpetually gray, the tomatoes wilted by frost before October first, the winter indoor life with its aching moments given to staring through windows at someone else's barren yard. Did one look east or west for a glimpse of mountain and sea? Something important was missing here.

I imagine my father conjuring the fig tree at the end of a long February day. March had yet to show itself, but April, also still hundreds of miles away confusedly east and west, eventually would melt the snow. Tony Posa had buried a fig tree under bales of straw in his back yard. If Tony Posa's fig survived the winter this year, why wouldn't one survive in the little piece of ground next to the garage? I see my father's eyes narrowing as the calculations run through his mind. How much sun would the tree really get, how much garden space would be lost, and how many years to a handful of figs? He begins seeing it—higher than the garage, its leaves spread on the roof, taller by far than Tony Posa's puny thing. He would water it every day and shield it from the cold with huge bales of straw.

What comes over a man, is it soul or mind—
That to no limits and bounds he can stay confined?

Thus Henry Ford's Igor, my father, resolves to challenge nature and try his own experiment with the elements.

Did he make my mother a happy woman that night?

As soon as it is warm enough for Tony Posa to roll the bales of straw away from his tree, he takes Tony a bottle of wine and returns home with a sprig of his own. He keeps it in a canning jar for more than a month, standing over it with thoughts more tangled than the tendril roots that finally appear in the brackish water. On a warm rainy night in late May I see my father digging in the yard, the jar at his side. He mixes sand from a bucket with the rich loam he has prepared, then finally puts the sprig in the ground, pats the soil all around, and steps back to behold his work. Day after day he waters it from an old coffee can, now and then turning the soil with a screw driver. For the longest time it looks like nothing more than a bare brown stick in the mud, my father, himself brown but showing the first signs of gray, with wordless soundings trying to tease some response from it.

Finally buds appear and then overnight the first small leaves. And what beautiful leaves, especially in miniature—their bright dark greens, soft and thick, deepening one of nature's lovely designs furled in on itself like an embryo. All through that first fig tree summer the unfurling goes on, the tiny leaves broadening into small garments perfectly cut to reveal the beauty in any Eve's form.

"Two more years," my father boasts, "and we'll have figs."

The chill always sets in long before September first, usually on one of those rare blue summer evenings when all seems right with the world. I catch my father gazing at the tree, his nerves on edge. Now what, when the cold weather comes on? He waits and watches as the leaves fall from the spindly tree, then on a late October Sunday morning he's in the yard again. First he bends the tree toward the ground, and ties it down with a rope. Around it he piles leaves and grass, and on top bushel-basketfuls of manure hauled in from the countryside, this heap eventually walled in by tightly stacked bales of straw.

My mother laughs. "Look at that monument. Like a castle with walls three feet thick. Maybe we should go live in there."

The first snows melt into the monument, and as the temperatures fall only the topmost bales are visible above the snow the winds have sculpted into a pyramidic swirl. What was he thinking about on sleepless nights? Bills to pay and too much work to do on the house after work. My mother unhappy and shrill. And a letter announcing that his mother, at ninety-one, is very ill. Will he ever return to Italy?

He now knew how way leads on to way, how the chain reactions of choice preclude returns. As the snows melt away from the base of his straw castle in early May, he stands next to it looking at the sky as if a God up there is someone he knows too well and doesn't trust. Then one day the impulse suddenly comes on. He marches into the yard, pulls the bales aside, and begins digging away at the mass of manure and rotting leaves. Finally he finds the cord, cuts it with a knife, and lifts the tree out—the main stem filthy in an ooze I dare not touch. He smiles as he points at tiny nubs of green already emerging along the stem.

Every day after work he waters it from a hose, then stands hands-on-hips as if waiting for it to grow in front of his eyes. It grows to five feet in that summer's heat, its leaves blossoming into a full green canopy, and the next winter the bales of straw are heaped so high the snow doesn't reach half of them. When spring finally returns he reaches into the muck and pulls it out again, tying it to a stake until it stands straight on its own. More nubs appear, the precious figs, only to shrink by mid-summer and fall off one by one. Tony Posa keeps coming over for a glass of wine, carrying with him a few of his own figs wrapped in a white linen cloth. "Next summer," my father says, "I'll be drinking your wine." "Maybe," Tony replies with a downward curl of his lips, "ifa you bury 'er good."

Bury a tree?

The next summer the tree is way over my head, and the figs—stiff and erect, like fat green raindrops—begin showing themselves inside the canopy of leaves. Eventually they began to turn purple in the August heat; they sag and one day finally fall into my father's hands. "Here," he says, as I take note of a drop of milk oozing from its stem, "like this." With his thumbs he splits it open for me to look inside. What do my teenage eyes see as I gaze into the pink seed-filled flesh? Something I had not seen before. My father lifts it closer to my lips. "Here, taste it." "Yuk," I say as I give it a few turns in my mouth and force it down.

Taste, and memory, naturally mature when given proper respect. For many years I walk right past the ripening figs, not suspecting that my father harbors a secret desire to hoard them all. My innocence does not allow me to care. The taste of figs is as un-American as my parents when they jabber in Italian in front of my friends. The difference in taste is widened by the distance between my boyhood and my father's youth, an age measurable by the miles separating the New World highways from the Old World paths. Rather desperately I want to look and feel American, and this requires further distancing. Much later—when I begin seeing my future in my past—I develop a desire for figs.

Where was my father looking—forward or back—when he made his decision to defy the northern elements? Like all of us, he was Janus-faced. And because there are roughly zones whose laws must be obeyed, he paid for getting cocky with the tree. The tree grew and grew, and the winter tower made of straw bales began to climb into the sky. Even as the tree began dwarfing him he stood tall next to it, as if to take full credit for its spectacular growth. Look at the work of my hands, his smile seemed to say whenever some figless friend dropped by. "I could sell these in a store. I could get rich with these."

He was rich until he, and the tree, got too big. The November day arrives when the tree has achieved such girth that it refuses to bow down easily for him. He stands in the yard looking at it, sullenly calculating, then gathers his tools and begins his sawing and hammering. When he is done he stands back to admire his new work, a wooden shack built around the tree from old boards. Then he begins lurking in neighborhoods in search of leaves, returning to the yard to stuff them in the shack. When late November temperatures foreshadow a winter unusually cold, he goes in search of straw bales to pile around the shack. Though in America the common faith is that everything looks up, the tree catches the cold and dies. Tony Posa's tree, only half as tall, survives. "Lika I tole you longa time ago," Tony says, "you gotta bury 'er good."

The following spring when Tony unburies his tree, my father, this time full of sullen respect for the American elements, starts all over again with a new cutting from it. From then on he trims the tree back to its proper bounds, digs a trench along the base of the garage, bends the tree into the trench, ties it down and buries it. When the snows come it looks enough like a grave to inspire me to imagine who might be buried there. For the first time I see my father dead, and when my mind reels away I see the grandfather in Italy I have never seen. It takes years more for me to see that I am buried there too.

My father's new tree eventually blossoms again, growing hardier as he cuts it back and buries it each year. But in the umbrage of the giant maples, elms, and oaks skyscraping the neighborhood the fig looks like a dwarfish weed. The limbs of the big trees, nature's monuments, crowd the heavens as if lifted to honor the gods of sky, the powerful grip their roots have on the earth too deep to be visible. The little fig reminds us of the presence of the underground life, its widespread tendril roots drawing the milk for its fruit from moisture on the earth's skin. Sensitive to the effects of frost that creeps up limbs like the hemlock Socrates drank, the fig seems more directly in touch with the life-and-death powers of earth.

We would have to fell a forest to produce the pulp necessary to properly celebrate this plant. It's not enough to note that trees, enduring in all but virtually lifeless cold, provide all manner of nuts, berries, and fruit, their wood shelter and heat, their foliage the very air we breathe. Standing there at the interstice between Sky and Earth, its natural art configuring the cross between our high yearning for transcendence and the limitations of our base humanity, my father's little fig tree grows in significance as I begin to see it against the ancient backgrounds detailed by Sir James Frazer and Joseph Campbell, those great loggers of arboreal rituals and myths. Though trees are said to be the source of home remedies for all manner of human ills—an infallible way to make hair grow long, for example, if we do as the Lkungen Indians of Vancouver Island do and mix fish oil with the pulverized fruit of the poplar *Populus trichocarpa;* though in Central Australia a man is said to be able to blind his enemy by rubbing himself against a tree that springs up on the spot where another blind man has died; though there is much to be said for (and against) that sacred tree in the grove of Aricia guarded by a grim figure, at once priest and murderer, trying to prevent his successor from plucking the golden bough that provides his challenger the right to rule; though many unlettered peoples deem trees animate and sensitive—the Ojibways reluctant to cut them down out of concern for inflicting pain, trees in many Chinese books bleeding and uttering cries when hacked or burned, and trees embodying the souls of dead ancestors in many parts of the world; though we learn that the great northern forests are the original Gothic "temples," embodiments of the Life-Spirit, and that the Swedes, Slavs, and Lithuanians were tree-worshippers before their conversion to the faith symbolized by the Calvary and Christmas trees, just as Romulus' sacred tree, also a fig, was worshipped in the Roman Forum until it was supplanted by the Cross; though that cunning adventurer-murderer Odysseus carved his marriage bed, peaceful stage of his odious dramas, out of the bole of a great olive tree, and Aeneas, his successor of sorts, also had to fetch a golden bough in order to achieve his triumphal journey to the underworld; and though several myths have at their center a drama featuring woman, serpent, man and tree, their setting a garden radiant in the sun, the Tree of Knowledge (and of Good and Evil) synonymous, in some of these myths, with the Tree of Immortal Life: Yet the tree looms largest when the great poets—among them Blake, Shelley, Yeats—figure the tree as the human mind, great-rooted blossomer of intellect, imagination, and song.

All this in my father's little fig tree, which I hereby name my family tree.

What seems obvious enough about family trees is the visible part, whose branches seem anatomically correct for delineating the proliferation of offspring from some (usually and merely conventionally) paternal main stem. When we genealogically draw them up the usual question is how far out to go—whether to include uncles and aunts, their children and their children's children too. At some point we prune, lest family members become as plentiful as leaves. But more significantly we cut the family tree off at ground level too, usually at the point where memory begins drawing a blank, the root system and its tangle of ganglia not only invisible but buried as if dead. If we start going down and out along the root-ganglia into dark history, beyond great-great grandpersons toward those strangers preceding them, ones with un-familiar names, we have to think in migratory terms: In my case Italians devolve into Romans, Goths and Huns, and certainly Greeks before them, all lineage an incestuous stew of "bloods" drawn by invading warmongers and wandering migrants. I find my family ganglia tangled with Saracen colonizers from North Africa, see their ancestors coming north across vast deserts to gaze at the Mediterranean, their grandparents perhaps from the bush country near some tropic river overgrown with jungle trees in which monkeys sit jeering down at us. I, child of southern Italians whom northerners jeeringly call *terroni*, earthlings, see my origin as a stew of Adam, Red Clay, and Eve, Life Force, brought into being by a chance lightning bolt that perfectly shocked some haplessly swimming string of DNA.

The mind reels, flies from that swamp.

So where are we now, we *terroni*, all so cut off from each other and our origins?

Last spring my mother, on her way north from Florida, visited her eighty-six year old sister in Chicago. Her brother, my Uncle Sam who lives in Skokie ten minutes away, could not manage the time to connect, and my mother, who never struck a final truce in their old sibling wars, didn't really mind that she probably would never, ever, see him again. I make an annual pilgrimage from Minnesota to Detroit to visit my sisters, but only twice in twenty-five years have they come my way. We love each other dearly, long distance. Since my parents now reside in Florida, we each see them once, maybe twice, a year. Recently I criticized a divorced ex-friend for trying to advance his new wife, also divorced, ahead of others more qualified for a job. "Bah! It all comes down to family!" he replied. Nepotism indeed—sans nephews, nieces, cousins, uncles or aunts, most of them out of sight and out of mind, like the old folks in nursing homes. Thus is family conveniently contracted into hybrid dwarf consisting of undivorced couple and kids still living in somebody's house.

We cannot tell a lie: It's the deals we've cut for ourselves that are chopping down the family tree. How many trees does it take to manufacture one car? As my father huddled in the January cold watching these American shores encroach on his immigrant boat, how many highways carved in the land did he see leading away from the sea? And after those highways drove him to the automobile plant in Detroit, did he see how the streets of that city, configured as a grid imposed on the radiating spokes of a wheel, were luring him farther from the taste of figs? How many times, contemplating the fires, did he pause to ask, "What am I doing here?" he perhaps aware only in those insane moments that it was too late to back out of the big Faustian deal America was making with the machine.

If family thrives in small spaces—villages, towns, and neighborhoods—how can the American machine, and the millions of accomplices who profit from its countless accessories, do anything but speed family on its way? What do we say to successful merchant saints who persistently whine about the family's decline? You reap what you sow?

After he retired from his factory work, my father retreated to his small spaces in back. There he finds some solace in the work of hands habituated to tending to the ground and its small growing things. House-bound, he does his faithful husbandry, at once quietly horrified by and grieving over the latest news from those all too familiar smaller nations where tribal wars and ethnic cleansing are the disorders of the day. In a century still going insane with blood-purification schemes— efficiently accomplished by proliferating and well-marketed machine-made arms—who needs more preoccupation with blood? And why believe in the Family of Woman and Man or any New World Order dream? Family's defunct. It's an arbitrary construct made up of a currently married couple, their current kids, and serial friends from here and there, without, thank you, too much of the regular round of holy-day to-do required of the old calendar. Tony Posa died a few winters ago, and his roots died too because his family buried him but not his tree.

A few years back I asked my brother-in-law, now divorced, for a cutting from my father's old fig. He, of English stock, had grown his own after unsuccessfully trying to become part of our peculiar tribe. I took my sprig home to Minnesota with me, dug up a bit of ground in the yard, and began watering it, amazed to see it keep shooting up after I took it inside to winter in the dining room. "I'm going to grow the first Minnesota fig," I boasted over the phone. "No," my father replied from his Florida house, "it's too cold way up there."

What comes over a man, is it soul or mind—
That to no limits and bounds he can stay confined?

That irrepressible urge—to test, meddle, expand, build highways into space—is all mine too, a blessing and curse. What we call Knowledge—as the Latin root for *educare*, "to lead forth," suggests—takes us away from home, much in the same way we thrive as biological creatures when we turn genetically outward rather than incestuously inward toward the familiar.

But it is not nostalgia that compels me down, in, and back toward a chthonic past too—toward brooks, fig trees, peasants, roots, all we associate with the natural world so slowly evolved and now so swiftly and inexorably becoming a wasteland. The field of forces that is *The* life is crossed by urges that impel us to fly entirely out of bounds while also pinning us to the ground in those rough zones whose laws must be obeyed. This cross, the human condition we all must bear, requires balance if we are to carry on. My father, small wheel in an enormous automobile plant, was himself a carrier of Mr. Ford's Faustian urge, an urge indifferent to the laws of balance and innocent of its role in creating the massive wreckage, material and human, of our century. Innocent of responsibilities beyond family, my father responsibly did his factory work. Not inclined to be like Mr. Ford and knowing there is no returning to the Old Country that impoverished him and his ancestors, he turned to his little garden plot. There, with his back to the factory and sky, he cultivated his own little wilderness, was Adam in his own New World garden, and, in the peace and quiet of his mind, had a love affair with his little tree.

Love—stressed, tattered, and hated—will persist, but what kind of beauty will survive nature's death? In the absence of political will, perhaps only private rituals expressing proper gestures remain for us to cultivate now. This past January my father turned ninety-six, and this past May I celebrated his birthday by unearthing my little Minnesota fig tree in back. He calls from Florida now and then, but his voice is small, he is so far away. His Old Country, surfacing mainly when he slips into Italian to express emotion or intimacy, also seems lost, blurred into the culture of the shopping mall without end. He tells me he's given up; he can't get a fig tree to grow in his arid Florida yard. He is almost gone.

I water my Minnesota fig tree sprig again, blossoming baton handed down through him from an ancient time, relic-totem of the greatest endangered species of all, the world's peasantries. It will be good work trying to keep that fig tree alive—work requiring thought about the quality of purposes. I keep seeing the milk-drop on the fig's stem, and resolve to observe the old calendar holidays. Each May Day unearthing and All Soul's Day reburial will be in honor of this ancient working man, five-foot five Promethean peasant hooked by the earth, now bowing, with his entire race, toward it, his quiet decent life still commanding, please, that we show some respect.

WITH GRATEFUL APPRECIATION

Bruno Borsari, Winona State University Professor Emeritus of Biology, for his dedication to agro-ecology and secrets of living organisms.

Kimberly Evenson, Winona State University Professor of Biology, for her careful contribution to my scientific understanding of plant life and its ways.

Orval Lund, Winona State Professor Emeritus of English, long-time colleague and friend, for important revision suggestions.

Jim Reynolds, Winona State Professor Emeritus Dean of Liberal Arts, for his encouragement and support.

Dara Syrkin, literary consultant, for helping me see my work more clearly.

John Toren, Nodin Press, for his "Macaroni" essays and book design advice.

Peter Wohlleben, for *The Hidden Life of Trees: What They Feel, How They Communicate—Discoveries from a Secret World*.

Richard Powers, for *Overstory,* his wonderful and learned novel about trees.

Matthew Hall, for *Plants as Persons: A Philosophic Botany*.

Craig Holdrege, for *Thinking Like a Plant: A Living Science for Life*.

Monica Gagliano, John C. Ryan, and Patricia Vieira, Editors, for *The Language of Plants: Science, Philosophy, Literature* (Minnesota, 2017).

David Beerling, for *The Emerald Planet*.